HEALTH CHOICES

KEEPING SAFE

Cath Senker

HODDER
Wayland

An imprint of Hodder Children's Books

Text copyright © Cath Senker 2004

Consultant: Jayne Wright
Design: Sarah Borny

Published in Great Britain in 2004
by Hodder Wayland, an imprint of
Hodder Children's Books

The publishers would like to thank the following for allowing
us to reproduce their pictures in this book:
Getty Images; 8, 13 (bottom) / Hodder Wayland Picture Library; 4, 5, 6, 7,
10, 11, 13 (top), 16, 17, 18, 19, 20, 21 / Zul Mukhida; 9, 14, 15

A catalogue record for this book is available from the British Library.

ISBN 07502 44976

Printed in China by WKT

Hodder Children's Books
A division of Hodder Headline Limited
338 Euston Road, London NW1 3BH

Contents

Why do people have accidents?

However young you are, you can learn to keep safe and help to keep others safe.

Remember that people can have an accident anywhere. Many accidents happen on the roads because there is so much traffic.

Sometimes children get hurt at school, often in the playground.

One out of every three accidents happens at home.

If someone has hurt themselves, always tell an adult straight away. Learn how to use the phone so you can call 999 for the emergency services if you need to.

If you dialled 999, what would you have to say? (Answer on page 22)

How should I cross the road safely?

The roads are dangerous because cars go very fast. It is hard for drivers to stop quickly. When you're out and about, watch out! When you need to cross the road, remember to 'Stop, look, listen and think'.

Use **pedestrian crossings** where you can. Wait until the cars stop, or the green man lights up, before you cross.

What is this girl doing to make sure she is safe crossing the road?

(Answer on page 23)

In the car, always wear a seat belt. Never undo it for any reason until the car has stopped and the driver says you can.

Sometimes drivers can't see people crossing the street. In the winter, it's dark coming home from school or the park. Make sure drivers can spot you. Try to wear light clothing. You can put **reflective** bands or stickers on your coat too.

What do I do if there's a fire?

It's very unlikely you'll ever be near a fire. Your home will be safer if you have a smoke alarm. If the alarm senses smoke from a fire it makes a very loud noise.

Make sure you know how to get out of your home quickly and safely in an emergency. If a fire starts, get out as fast as you can. Call 999 from a neighbour's phone.

If a fire starts, in what order should you do these things?
1. Ask for the fire service
2. Call 999
3. Get out of the house quickly
4. Give your address

(Answer on page 23)

Ask for the

fire service. When

you are connected,

give your address.

Never play with matches, candles or

anything else that burns. You could burn

yourself or even start a fire.

How do I keep safe when I'm out?

When you're out, stay with the older person you're with. Do you know your full name, address and phone number? Try to learn them in case you ever need to tell someone.

> **Remember: never go off anywhere with a person you don't know.**

If you do get lost, call the police. Ask an adult in a shop or a parent with children to help you. You can call 999 from a phone box or a mobile phone.

What safety items is this cyclist wearing and why? (Answer on page 23)

If you like to cycle, scoot or skate, get ahead – get a helmet! A helmet protects your head. If you fall off, it can save you from a nasty injury.

Why should I learn to swim?

It could save your life. If you fall into water by accident you are more likely to be able to save yourself.

Take care by rivers, ponds and lakes. Stand away from the edge. It could be muddy and slippery and you might fall in. Stay safe and sound – keep your feet on the ground.

In the sea there are strong **currents**. They can pull you out to sea when you are swimming. Always go in the sea with an adult. Stay and play where you can stand up – even if you can swim.

What are the children in both these pictures doing to keep safe? (Answer on page 23)

Do I really need sun cream?

Yes you do! It's fun to play in the sun. A little sunshine does you good. The sun's rays are very strong though. They can burn your skin. The sun is strongest around midday.

Stay cool in the shade during the hottest part of the day.

If you have blonde hair and pale skin, you have a high risk of sunburn.

If you don't want to burn use sun cream with at least **factor** 15 protection. Cover your shoulders and thighs.

Remember that hat! It protects your head and your face from the sun's rays. If you burn it really hurts! It harms your skin too.

How do we make food safe to eat?

Make sure you wash your hands before you eat so you don't get dirt and germs on your food.

Raw foods like fruit and salad vegetables often have dirt and germs on them. They may have been sprayed with chemicals to help them grow. Be sure to wash them before you start munching. Then they will be safe for you to enjoy.

Keep fresh foods in the fridge so they do not go bad quickly. Food that has gone off can make you ill.

It's fun to eat with friends, but touching other people's food is rude! Sharing food can mean sharing germs too. Keep pets away from your food because they carry germs. Don't let the dog get your dinner!

I've cut myself. What do I do?

Ouch! If you cut or scratch yourself badly, blood comes out. If this happens, tell an adult. The adult will need to wash the cut.

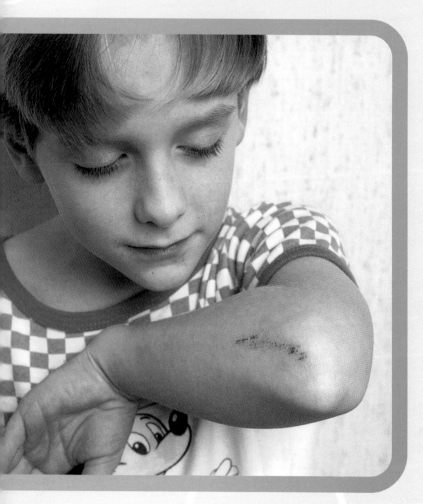

If it is a big cut, you might need some *antiseptic* cream. Stop the bleeding and keep it clean with a bandage or plaster. This will help it to heal faster.

If it's a really deep cut, you may need to go to hospital. The wound can be stitched or glued by a nurse or doctor.

You can't put a plaster on a bruise. The bleeding is under the skin so it won't help. The bruise will heal by itself.

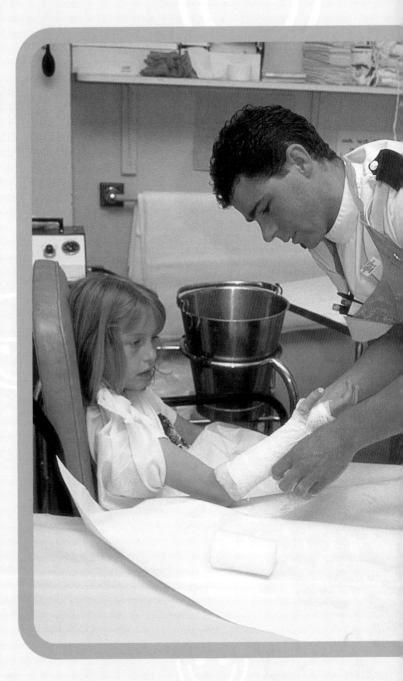

How do I keep safe in the kitchen?

If you're helping in the kitchen, keep your fingers away from sharp knives and machines like **food processors**.

There are a lot of hot things in the kitchen. Be very careful if you're stirring food on the hob. Keep away from the hot oven and the steaming kettle.

When using sharp knives keep your fingers out of the way and always use a chopping board.

Burns are really painful. If you burn yourself, go to the sink and run cold water over the sore part. Tell an adult straight away. Keep the water running for 15 minutes – that's a long time! If you're out and about and there's no tap put the burnt part in cold water or milk.

Glossary and index

Answers to questions:

P.5 When you call 999, you need to say which service you want. In this case you need to ask for an ambulance. You will then be connected to the ambulance service. The person you speak to will need to know your name, address and phone number, and what the problem is.

P.6   To make sure she is safe crossing the road, the girl is holding her carer's hand, standing away from the edge of the kerb and looking left and right to see if there is any traffic coming.

P.9   If a fire starts you should do these things:

1 Get out of the house quickly

2 Call 999

3 Ask for the fire service

4 Give your address

P.11 The cyclist is wearing a helmet to protect her head and reflective bands so that car drivers can see her clearly.

P.13 The girl by the waterfall is staying back from the edge and is close to an adult. The girl in the sea is staying in shallow water, and is wearing arm-bands to help her to float.

Finding out more

Books to read:

Bad Days for Thomas and his Friends
by Christopher Awdry (Railway Safety, 2001)

Kids to the Rescue! First Aid Techniques for Kids
by Maribeth Boelts (Parenting Press, 2003)

More Bad Days for Thomas and his Friends
by Christopher Awdry (Railway Safety, 2001)

Staying Safe in Playgrounds; Staying Safe Near Fire;
Staying Safe Near Water; Staying Safe on Bikes
all by Maribeth Boelts (Franklin Watts, 1998)

What About Health? Hygiene
by Cath Senker (Hodder Wayland, 2001)

Creating a Safe Journey to School (video)
from Sustrans, 35 King Street, Bristol
BS1 4DZ; Tel: 0117 915 0100
Email: schools@sustrans.org.uk